Texas Assessment Preparation

Grade 2

TEXAS
JOURNEYs

TEXAS
WRITE
SOURCE

 HOUGHTON MIFFLIN HARCOURT

Contents

How To Use This Book

This book will help you practice for the Texas reading and writing tests. The book is in four parts: Reading, Writing, Revising, and Editing.

- **Reading**   This part has passages in different genres. A **genre** is a type of writing, such as fiction or poetry. **Tips** help you as you read the passages and answer the questions.

- **Writing**   This part has writing prompts that tell you what to write about. There are also samples of other students' writing that show you how to write well.

- **Revising and Editing**   These parts help you practice ways to make your writing better.

Get Credit for Your Answers

- **Multiple-Choice Questions**   On your test page, fill in each correct answer bubble completely. Check your work. Be sure you have not missed a question or filled in more than one bubble for a question.

- **Writing Prompts**   You may use your own paper when you write your first draft. Make all your changes on this draft. For your final draft, write as clearly as you can. Be sure that your final draft is no more than one page long.

4

Read the Signs

As you work through this book, you will see the signs and
symbols below. Be sure you understand what they mean.

Read this selection.	Words in a box tell you what to do. Read them carefully to make sure you understand.
In paragraph 10, the word <u>genre</u> means —	Underlined words in a question mean the same words are underlined in the passage.
What is the **BEST** way to revise sentence 7?	Words like **BEST** mean you should pick the answer that makes the most sense.
GO ON →	This arrow means you should go on to the next page.
STOP	This stop sign means you should put your pencil down.

Texas Assessment
Practice

Fiction

Genre Overview

Fiction is a kind of story that is made up, or not real. A fiction story has at least one **character**, at least one **setting**, and a **plot**. The author puts them together in a way that will best tell the story.

As you read fiction, look for the **characters**. They are the people or animals in the story. Think about what they think, do, and say.

The **setting** is the place and time in which the story happens. To identify the setting, ask yourself where and when the story takes place.

The **plot** is what happens in a story. The plot is made up of events that happen in order.

Sometimes the story includes a moral, or **theme**. The moral is the message, or lesson, the author wants to share with the reader. In a fable like *The Lion and the Mouse*, the author includes a moral at the end of the story.

An author of fiction may not always explain the ideas or events in the story. The reader may have to **make inferences**. Readers do this by using clues from the text to figure out what the author does not say.

As you read, look at the pictures in the story. The words and the pictures work together to help you understand what you are reading.

A word may have more than one meaning. Look at the words around that word to help you figure out what it means.

Fiction

> **Read this selection. Then answer the questions that follow it.**
> **Fill in the circle of the correct answer.**

The Lion and the Mouse

1   It was a hot summer day in the jungle. A lion lay napping under a big tree. Suddenly, a mouse ran over the lion's tail. The lion woke up. He was very angry.

2   He grabbed the mouse by the tail. "How dare you disturb my rest!" he shouted. "I'm going to gobble you up for dinner!"

3   The mouse begged the lion to let him go. "Please don't hurt me, King Lion!" said the mouse. "If you set me free, maybe someday I can help you."

4   The lion thought that was a funny idea. "How could someone as small as you help a huge lion like me?" He looked at the tiny mouse and laughed. "You're even too small to make a good meal." So he let the mouse run away.

Tip

Why does the lion laugh at the mouse? Keep reading to find out how the lion's feelings toward the mouse change.

GO ON

Grade 2: Fiction

5   A few days later, the lion was out looking for food. He stepped into a hunter's net that had been covered by leaves. His paws got caught in the net, and he was trapped.

6   "I'm stuck! Help me!" roared the lion. But the other animals did not want to rescue the lion. They were afraid he might eat them. They walked right past him and pretended not to hear him.

7   The mouse, however, ran to help. He climbed on the lion's paws and went to work. The mouse chewed through the net and set the lion free.

8   "Thank you! You saved me," said the lion. "I will never again judge anyone by his or her size."

Tip

Think about the theme of the story. What lesson does the author want to share with the reader?

GO ON

1 Read the words in the web.

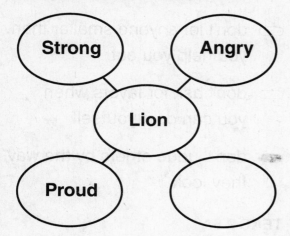

Which word belongs in the web?

◯ Stubborn

◯ Silly

⬤ Grateful

TEKS 2.9B

2 The word <u>gobble</u> in paragraph 2 means—

⬤ eat quickly

◯ cry like a turkey

◯ grab from someone

TEKS 2.5B

Tip
Sometimes a word has more than one meaning. To figure out the correct meaning, look at the other words in the sentence.

3 Which event happened before the lion set the mouse free?

◯ The lion called for help.

◯ The mouse woke up the lion.

⬤ The lion got caught in the net.

TEKS RC-2(E)

Tip
What is the order of events in the story?

GO ON ➡

Name _____ Date _____

4 Based on paragraph 7, the reader knows that the mouse is—

- ○ afraid
- ● kind
- ○ hungry

TEKS RC-2(D)

Tip
Look for clues in the paragraph to help answer the question.

5 Based on the illustration and paragraph 7, how does the mouse help the lion?

- ● He uses his teeth to bite through the net.
- ✗ He uses his claws to pull the net away from the lion.
- ✗ He finds another animal to free the lion from the net.

TEKS 2.16

Tip
Reread paragraph 7 and try to picture what happens. How does the illustration help?

6 The theme of this selection is—

- ○ don't let anyone smaller than you help you out
- ○ don't ask for favors when you can do it yourself
- ● don't judge others by the way they look

TEKS 2.6A

Grade 2: Fiction

Name _____ Date _____

TEKS 2.3B, 2.5A, 2.10, 2.11, RC-2(D), RC-2(E)

Literary Nonfiction

Genre Overview

Literary nonfiction tells about real people and events. It gives facts and details about a **subject**. The subject is the person or the thing the selection is about. **Facts** are statements or ideas that are true. The author usually writes about events in the order in which they happened.

Sometimes part of a selection may confuse you. If something doesn't make sense, stop and ask yourself questions about the text. Use facts and details from the selection to support your answers. For example, if you are not sure when an event happens, think about when other events happen.

As you read, you might see words that you do not know. Sometimes these words have a beginning part, or **prefix**, that you do know. They may also have an ending part, or **suffix**, that you recognize. For example, the prefix *dis-* means "not." If you do not like the color blue, then you dislike it.

You may also find that some words and phrases have more than one meaning. For example, if you say "cut it out," you are asking someone to stop what he or she is doing. You are not asking someone to cut something.

13

Name _____ Date _____

TEKS 2.3B, 2.5A, 2.10, 2.11,
RC-2(D), RC-2(E)

Literary Nonfiction

Read this selection. Then answer the questions that follow it.
Fill in the circle of the correct answer.

Grandma Moses

1   Can you imagine never taking an art
lesson but becoming a world-famous painter?
That's what happened to a tiny gray-haired
grandmother. Her name was Anna Mary
Robertson Moses. People called her
Grandma Moses.

2   Grandma Moses liked to make pictures. First,
Grandma Moses loved to sew pictures on cloth.
Then, as she got older, her hands began to hurt
when she sewed. So Grandma Moses decided
to paint instead. She became a painter in 1935.
She was 75 years old!

> **Tip**
> Think about the order of
> events in the selection.

3   She painted her first picture on a piece of
canvas. She used house paint. At first she
copied pictures from postcards. Then she
began to paint things she remembered from
her childhood.

4   When Grandma Moses was a young girl, she
saw people using the sap from maple trees to
make syrup and sugar. "Sugaring off" is a
special name for what happens when sap is
collected from maple trees and turned into
maple sugar and syrup.

Grade 2: Literary Nonfiction

5   Grandma Moses painted many pictures about sugaring off. She showed people carrying buckets of sap from maple trees in the background. She showed the boiling pots of sap and the sugar shack. Grandma Moses added <u>beautiful</u> touches of glitter to her paintings. The snow in her pictures would <u>dance</u> and sparkle.

6   Grandma Moses left behind over 1,600 paintings. In fact, she painted 25 pictures in the last year of her life, when she was 100 years old!

Tip
Is this selection fiction or nonfiction? Look back at the selection. Was Grandma Moses a real person?

GO ON

Name _____ Date _____

TEKS 2.3B, 2.5A, 2.10, 2.11,
RC-2(D), RC-2(E)

1 This selection is nonfiction because it—

⬭ is about a made-up person

⬭ is about a real person

⬭ never really happened

TEKS 2.10

2 Which sentence tells the reader that Grandma Moses did not paint all of her life?

⬭ *She became a painter in 1935.*

⬭ *She painted her first picture on a piece of canvas.*

⬭ *Grandma Moses painted many pictures about sugaring off.*

TEKS RC-2(D)

Tip
Think about what is being described in each answer choice.

3 Which paragraph tells what Grandma Moses used for paint?

⬭ Paragraph 1

⬭ Paragraph 2

⬭ Paragraph 3

TEKS 2.3B

Tip
Reread the paragraphs to find the details that answer the question.

GO ON

Grade 2: Literary Nonfiction

Name _____ Date _____

4 In paragraph 5, the word <u>beautiful</u> means—

- ◯ without beauty
- ◯ full of beauty
- ◯ not more than one beauty

TEKS 2.5A

5 How can snow <u>dance</u> in paragraph 5?

- ◯ There were shoes kicking the snow.
- ◯ The snow was melting.
- ◯ The sparkle made it look like it moved.

TEKS 2.11

Tip
The word <u>dance</u> describes what the snow looks like. It doesn't mean it is really dancing.

6 Read the chart and answer the question below.

Grandma Moses sewed pictures on cloth.
↓
Her hands began to hurt.
↓
↓
She copied pictures from postcards.

Which event belongs in the chart?

- ◯ She became a painter.
- ◯ She saw people collect sap.
- ◯ She painted at the age of 100.

TEKS RC-2(E)

Tip
This chart is about the order of events. Think about which event is missing.

Grade 2: Literary Nonfiction

Expository Text

Genre Overview

Expository text gives facts and information about the topic, or subject, of a text. When you read expository text, look for the main idea. The **main idea** is often a sentence that tells what the text is mostly about. The author of expository text gives details and facts to support the main idea.

Authors write expository text for a certain **purpose**, or reason. They might give information about a topic. Or, they might explain how to do something.

Expository text may include directions or steps to follow. The directions or steps are usually organized in a **sequence**. This means the information is given in a specific order.

Expository text may have **text features** such as illustrations, captions, bold print, or headings. These features can help you find or learn new information. For example, the heading of a section tells you what kind of information is in the section.

GO ON

Expository Text

> **Read this selection. Then answer the questions that follow it.**
> **Fill in the circle of the correct answer.**

Feeding Birds

1   Different kinds of birds look for food in different places. That's why there are many kinds of bird feeders.

Feeders in the Air

2   Hummingbirds and orioles eat from hummingbird feeders. This kind of feeder holds sugar water. The birds sip the water through a tube. Hummingbird feeders hang from a hook.

3   A second kind of feeder is a post feeder. It holds seeds. The feeder sits on top of a tall post off the ground. Birds like to perch on the feeder. You might see robins, woodpeckers, and doves sitting on it.

Feeders on the Ground

4   Many birds eat from the ground. You can feed them from a tray feeder. A tray feeder is flat like a plate. Just put some seeds, popcorn, or bread in the tray on the ground. Then watch the sparrows, wrens, and blue jays gather around.

> **Tip**
>
> The title of this selection is *Feeding Birds*. This is the topic. Which sentence gives the main idea of paragraph 4?

GO ON

Feeders You Can Make

5   For a fun craft project, try making a pinecone bird feeder. With an adult's help, you can make this special treat for the birds in your neighborhood.

6   First, tie a long piece of string to the top of a pinecone. Spread peanut buttter on the pinecone. Next, pour birdseed onto a plate. Roll the pinecone in the birdseed. Your pinecone feeder is done!

7   For your next feeder, try using sunflower seeds. Many birds like sunflower seeds, especially cardinals, chickadees, and goldfinches. Always ask an adult to help when you hang your feeder from a tree.

Tip
Think about how text features help you find information. What does the heading tell you?

GO ON ➡

1 Read the information in the chart. Use it to answer the question.

Type of Bird Feeder	Types of Birds
Hummingbird feeder Post feeder	Hummingbirds, orioles
Tray feeder	Sparrows, wrens, blue jays

Which birds should be added to the chart?

◯ Orioles, wrens, sparrows

◯ Robins, woodpeckers, doves

◯ Hummingbirds, blue jays

TEKS 2.14B

Tip
Each paragraph has different facts. Which paragraph has facts about post feeders?

2 What is the main idea of *Feeding Birds*?

◯ There are many different kinds of birds.

◯ Birds get food in different ways.

◯ Some birds are easier to feed than others.

TEKS 2.14A

3 Which information can be found under **Feeders on the Ground**?

◯ *Hummingbird feeders hang from a hook.*

◯ *Birds like to perch on the feeder.*

◯ *You can feed them from a tray feeder.*

TEKS 2.14D

Tip
This question asks about a specific section. Look under the heading to find the answer.

GO ON ➤

Grade 2: Expository Text

Name _____ Date _____

4 Which feeder has a tube for birds to sip through?

○ Hummingbird feeder

○ Post feeder

○ Tray feeder

TEKS 2.15B

Tip
Look at the picture of the bird sipping through the tube. Reread the selection. Which feeder is it?

5 The author wrote about a pinecone feeder to—

○ give facts about pinecones

○ describe how to get birds to eat

○ explain how to make a feeder

TEKS 2.14A

Tip
The section title is a clue. Ask yourself what the author is trying to tell you.

6 In paragraph 6, what is the last step you should do when making a pinecone feeder?

○ Roll the pinecone in the birdseed.

○ Tie the string to the top of the pinecone.

○ Spread peanut butter on the pinecone.

TEKS 2.14C

Grade 2: Expository Text

Poetry

Genre Overview

Poetry can tell a story, or it can describe something. Poetry can rhyme or have words that repeat. A poem can have a strong beat, or rhythm. Poetry sometimes uses the sounds of words to describe feelings.

A poem **rhymes** when two or more lines end with the same sound, such as *pool* and *rule*. A poem has **rhythm** when the words make up a pattern of beats, like the beat of a drum. A poem has **repetition** when words, phrases, rhymes, and even lines are used more than once.

Some poetry tells a story. Like fiction, it can have characters, a setting, and plot events.

As you read, you may find **synonyms**, or words with almost the same meaning. You may also find **antonyms**, or words that have opposite meanings. For example, *loud* and *noisy* are synonyms. *Silent* and *noisy* are antonyms.

Poetry

Name _____ Date _____

Read this selection. Then answer the questions that follow it.
Fill in the circle of the correct answer.

A New School

1   Today was my first day
    at the new school in my new town.

3   Mom said, "Emily, wear a smile!"
    But all I could do was <u>frown</u>.

5   I sat on the new bus all alone,
    my new backpack by my side.
    Would I make friends at this new school?
    I wondered and I sighed.

    At the next bus stop,
10 a girl sat next to me.
    She was in my new class.
    And her name was Emily!

    When the bus stopped at the new school,
    I met her friends Kay, James, and Brad.

15 Why was I so worried?
    A new school isn't all that bad.

Tip

This poem tells a story. Stop every few lines to say what happened in your own words.

Tip

Find the repeated word in the poem. What effect does that have?

GO ON

24

Grade 2: Poetry

Name _____ Date _____

1 The author repeats the word *new* to—

○ show how things feel to Emily

○ describe the school

○ explain why Emily is late

TEKS 2.7

Tip
Reread the poem. Focus on the lines that repeat the word. How does Emily feel?

2 In line 3, the phrase "wear a smile" means—

○ never smile at others

○ keep a smile on your face

○ don't smile if you can help it

TEKS 2.11

3 Why does Emily frown?

○ Emily has too many new friends to sit with.

○ Emily doesn't have anything new to wear.

○ Emily is worried about going to a new school.

TEKS 2.9B

Tip
What happens in the poem to make Emily frown? Read the end of the poem to see how Emily's feelings change.

4 Which word from the poem means the opposite of <u>frown</u>?

○ *smile*

○ *wondered*

○ *worried*

TEKS 2.5C

GO ON

Grade 2: Poetry

Name _____ Date _____

5 Emily feels better about the new school because of—

○ her new backpack

○ the school bus ride

○ her new friends

TEKS RC-2(D)

Tip
What helps Emily change the way she feels at the end of the poem?

6 What happens at the next bus stop?

○ Mom tells Emily to smile.

○ The other Emily gets on.

○ Emily sits alone.

TEKS RC-2(E)

Reading
PRACTICE

TEKS 2.3B, 2.5A, 2.5B, 2.5C,
2.6A, 2.9B, 2.11,
RC-2(D), RC-2(E)

> **Read this selection. Then answer the questions that follow it.**
> **Fill in the circle of the correct answer.**

Mr. Putter & Tabby Pour the Tea
by Cynthia Rylant

Mr. Putter

1   Before he got his fine cat, Tabby, Mr. Putter lived all alone. In the mornings he had no one to share his English muffins. In the afternoons he had no one to share his tea. And in the evenings there was no one Mr. Putter could tell his stories to. And he had the most <u>wonderful</u> stories to tell.

2   All day long as Mr. Putter clipped his roses and fed his tulips and watered his trees, Mr. Putter wished for some company. He had warm muffins to eat. He had good tea to pour. And he had wonderful stories to tell. Mr. Putter was tired of living alone. Mr. Putter wanted a cat. Mr. Putter went to the shelter.

3   "Have you any cats?" he asked the shelter man.

4   "We have a fat gray one, a thin black one, and an old yellow one," said the man.

5   "Did you say old?" asked Mr. Putter.

GO ON

Grade

© Houghton Mifflin

Reading
PRACTICE

Name _____   Date _____

TEKS 2.3B, 2.5A, 2.5B, 2.5C,
2.6A, 2.9B, 2.11,
RC-2(D), RC-2(E)

6   The shelter man brought Mr. Putter the old yellow cat. Its bones creaked, its fur was thinning, and it seemed a little deaf. Mr. Putter creaked, his hair was thinning, and he was a little deaf, too. So he took the old yellow cat home. He named her Tabby. And that is how their life began.

Mr. Putter and Tabby

7   Tabby loved Mr. Putter's tulips. She was old, and beautiful things meant more to her. She would rub past all the yellow tulips. Then she would roll past all the red tulips. Then she would take her bath among all the pink tulips. Mr. Putter clipped roses while Tabby bathed.

8   In the mornings Mr. Putter and Tabby liked to share an English muffin. Mr. Putter ate his with <u>jam</u>. Tabby ate hers with cream cheese. In the afternoons Mr. Putter and Tabby liked to share tea. Mr. Putter took his with sugar. Tabby took hers with cream. And in the evenings they sat by the window, and Mr. Putter told stories. He told the most wonderful stories. Each story made Tabby purr.

9   On summer days they warmed their old bones together in the sun. On fall days they took long walks through the trees. And on winter days they turned the <u>opera</u> up *very* loud.

GO ON

rcourt Publishing Company

10   After a while it seemed as if they had always lived together. Tabby knew just what Mr. Putter was going to do next. Mr. Putter knew just where Tabby was going to sleep next.

11   In the mornings each looked for the other as soon as they opened their eyes. And at night each looked for the other as their eyes were closing. Mr. Putter could not remember life without Tabby. Tabby could not remember life without Mr. Putter.

12   They lived among their tulips and trees. They ate their muffins. They poured their tea. They turned up the opera, and enjoyed the most perfect company of all – each other.

Grade 2: Reading Practice

Reading

PRACTICE

Name _____ Date _____

TEKS 2.3B, 2.5A, 2.5B, 2.5C,
2.6A, 2.9B, 2.11, RC-2(D),
RC-2(E)

1 Read the words in the web.

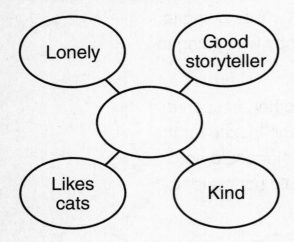

Which of these belongs in the middle of the web?

- Mr. Putter
- Tabby
- the shelter man

TEKS 2.9B

2 The word <u>wonderful</u> in paragraph 1 means—

- without wonder
- full of wonder
- not long

TEKS 2.5A

3 Tabby is—

- a fat gray cat
- a thin black cat
- an old yellow cat

TEKS 2.3B

4 Which sentence from the selection shows why Mr. Putter chose Tabby?

- *Mr. Putter wanted a cat.*
- *The shelter man brought Mr. Putter the old yellow cat.*
- *Mr. Putter creaked, his hair was thinning, and he was a little deaf, too.*

TEKS RC-2(D)

GO ON

5 What are paragraphs 1 and 2 mostly about?

⬭ Mr. Putter was lonely so he wanted a cat.

⬭ Mr. Putter clipped his roses and fed his tulips.

⬭ Mr. Putter had warm muffins and good tea.

TEKS RC-2(E)

6 In paragraph 8, the word <u>jam</u> means almost the same as—

⬭ butter

⬭ jelly

⬭ cheese

TEKS 2.5C

7 In paragraph 9, the phrase "warmed their old bones" means—

⬭ sat in the sun

⬭ cooked some ham bones

⬭ made a campfire

TEKS 2.11

8 In paragraph 9, which word helps the reader know that <u>opera</u> is something you listen to?

⬭ *together*

⬭ *trees*

⬭ *loud*

TEKS 2.5B

9 Mr. Putter and Tabby spend time together because they—

⬭ like to take walks

⬭ want to open a bakery

⬭ enjoy being together

TEKS RC-2(D)

10 This selection teaches the reader that—

⬭ we all need friends

⬭ cats make better pets than dogs

⬭ people should grow tulips

TEKS 2.6A

Grade 2: Reading Practice

Name _____ Date _____

Reading
PRACTICE

TEKS 2.3B, 2.5A, 2.5B,
2.5C, 2.10, 2.11, 2.14C,
RC-2(D), RC-2(E)

**Read this selection. Then answer the questions that follow it.
Fill in the circle of the correct answer.**

Robert Fulton

by Jennifer Boothroyd

A Talented Artist

1   Robert was born on November 14, 1765, in Pennsylvania. As a young man, he worked for a jewelry maker. Robert painted very well. His job was to paint tiny pictures on necklaces and rings.

2   Robert wanted to paint better. He went to Great Britain to study painting with a famous painter.

3   Robert became a good painter. But he was not good enough to earn much money selling his art.

Using His Talent

4   Robert thought of another way to use his art skills. He decided to design <u>useful</u> things. His ideas would fix problems and make things better. He hoped to sell his ideas. His first idea was to make transportation faster.

5   Robert designed canals. Boats on canals could travel faster than wagons on roads. They could deliver goods more quickly.

GO ON

Name _____ Date _____

Reading
PRACTICE

TEKS 2.3B, 2.5A, 2.5B,
2.5C, 2.10, 2.11, 2.14C,
RC-2(D), RC-2(E)

6   Robert had seen plans for an underwater boat. This gave Robert another idea.

7   Robert designed a submarine to sink warships. He took his new idea to France.

8   Robert talked to the French leaders about his invention. They did not like how it worked.

Robert's Partner

9   In France, Robert met an American named Robert Livingston. Robert Livingston knew the United States was <u>growing</u> quickly. The country needed a better way to bring people and goods to the new cities. He asked Robert Fulton to design and build a steamboat.

10   Other people had tried to build steamboats. But none of them worked very well.

11   Robert studied old steamboat plans. He used the best ideas to design his boat.

12   He connected two paddle wheels to the engine. The wheels turn and the paddles <u>push</u> the boat through the water.

13   Robert tested his new steamboat. It worked!

Grade 2: Reading Practice

Name _____ Date _____

Reading
PRACTICE

TEKS 2.3B, 2.5A, 2.5B,
2.5C, 2.10, 2.11, 2.14C,
RC-2(D), RC-2(E)

Success in the United States

14   The partners moved to the United States. Robert made a steamboat to travel the Hudson River. It would travel from New York City to Albany, New York. This trip usually took four days. To be a success, Robert's ship had to travel faster. He added a more powerful engine to this steamboat.

15   Robert's boat finished the <u>trip</u> in less than a day and a half. His innovation worked.

16   Robert's steamboat became very popular. He designed more steamboats to travel on other rivers in the United States.

Innovation

17   Many of Robert's inventions were not his own ideas. Robert's steamboat was not the first steamboat invented. But through innovation, he improved it. Robert took a good idea and made it better.

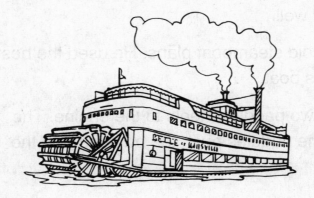

Grade 2: Reading Practice

Name _____ Date _____

1 You can tell that this selection is nonfiction because—

○ it tells a true story

○ it has a lesson or message

○ its lines end in rhyming words

TEKS 2.10

2 In paragraph 4, the word <u>useful</u> means—

○ costly

○ helpful

○ empty

TEKS 2.5A

3 From the information in paragraph 4, the reader can tell that Robert—

○ had a lot of time

○ wanted to help people

○ did not like painting jewelry

TEKS RC-2(D)

4 What happens after Robert takes his new idea to France?

○ Robert designs canals.

○ The French do not like it.

○ Robert studies art in Great Britain.

TEKS 2.14C

5 In paragraph 9, what does the word <u>growing</u> mean?

○ Learning more

○ Getting older

○ Spreading out

TEKS 2.11

6 Which paragraph tells how Robert makes his steamboat?

○ Paragraph 11

○ Paragraph 12

○ Paragraph 13

TEKS 2.3B

GO ON ▶

Grade 2: Reading Practice

Name _____ Date _____

7 Which word means the opposite of
<u>push</u> in paragraph 12?

⬭ Spin

⬭ Pull

⬭ Close

TEKS 2.5C

8 In paragraph 15, <u>trip</u> means—

⬭ journey

⬭ fall

⬭ mistake

TEKS 2.5B

9 Robert's steamboat was a success
because it—

⬭ traveled on rivers and oceans

⬭ was the only steamboat in the
United States

⬭ helped people and goods
travel faster

TEKS RC-2(D)

10 What is paragraph 17 mostly
about?

⬭ Robert invented many things.
Most were other people's
ideas that he made better.

⬭ Other people built steamboats.
Robert did not build one.

⬭ Robert thought of many good
ideas. So did other people.

TEKS RC-2(E)

11 Read the chart and answer the
question below.

Fiction	Nonfiction
Has made-up characters	

Which one belongs in the chart?

⬭ Has stage directions

⬭ Uses clues to solve a mystery

⬭ Tells about real people

TEKS 2.10

Grade 2: Reading Practice

> **Read this selection. Then answer the questions that follow it.**
> **Fill in the circle of the correct answer.**

From Seed to Plant
by Gail Gibbons

1   Most plants make seeds. A seed contains the beginning of a new plant.

2   Seeds are different shapes, sizes and colors.

3   All seeds grow into the same kind of plant that made them.

4   Many plants grow flowers. Flowers are where most seeds begin.

5   Some seeds fall to the ground around the <u>base</u> of the plant where they will grow.

6   Some pods or fruits open and the seeds pop out. Sometimes, when birds eat berries, they drop the seeds.

Grade 2: Reading Practice

7   Other seeds fall into streams, ponds, rivers or the ocean. There, they travel on the water until they stick to dirt along a shore.

8   The wind scatters seeds. Some seeds have fluff on them that lets them float to the ground like tiny parachutes. Others have wings that spin as they fall.

9   Animals help scatter seeds, too. They hide acorns and nuts in the ground. Some seeds have hooks that stick to the fur of animals or people's clothes. Later, they drop off onto the ground.

10   A flower bed or vegetable garden is beautiful! Seeds are planted to grow in the gardens.

11   The seeds come in small envelopes or boxes. Directions explain how to plant the seeds and care for the plants.

12   A seed will not sprout until certain things happen. First it must be on or in the soil. Then it needs rain to soak the seed and soften its seed coat.

13   When the sun shines and warms the ground, the seed coat breaks open and the seed begins to grow. This is called germination. A root grows down into the soil. The root takes in water and minerals from the soil for food.

14   Up grows a shoot. Green leaves grow up from the shoot toward the sun.

15   The plant grows bigger and bigger. The leaves make food for the plant from the water and minerals in the soil, the sunlight, and the air all around the plant.

16   Finally, the plant is full-grown. Buds on the plant open into flowers where new seeds will grow.

17   Many of the foods people eat are seeds, fruits and pods. They are full of nutrition, vitamins and minerals and … they are tasty, too!

Grade 2: Reading Practice

1 All seeds grow into—

- ⬭ fruits and vegetables

- ⬭ flowers with pretty colors

- ⬭ the same kind of plant that made them

TEKS 2.14B

2 Most seeds begin in—

- ⬭ trees

- ⬭ rivers

- ⬭ flowers

TEKS 2.14B

3 Based on the illustration, an acorn will grow into—

- ⬭ a sunflower

- ⬭ an oak tree

- ⬭ a seed

TEKS 2.15B

4 In paragraph 5, which words help explain what <u>base</u> means?

- ⬭ *of the plant*

- ⬭ *fall to the ground*

- ⬭ *they will grow*

TEKS 2.5B

5 What is the topic of this selection?

- ⬭ Seeds

- ⬭ Nature

- ⬭ Gardens

TEKS 2.14A

Grade 2: Reading Practice

6 Read the sentences in the chart.

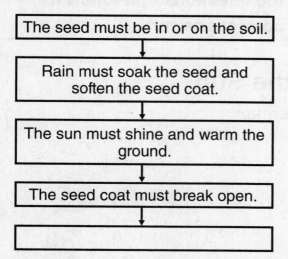

| The seed must be in or on the soil. |
| Rain must soak the seed and soften the seed coat. |
| The sun must shine and warm the ground. |
| The seed coat must break open. |
| |

Which sentence should be added to the chart?

⬭ The seed is planted in the ground.

⬭ The seed begins to grow.

⬭ The seed is blown away by the wind.

TEKS 2.14C

7 What is the main idea of paragraph 13?

⬭ why the sun shines

⬭ what germination is

⬭ what minerals are

TEKS 2.14A

8 The author wrote this selection to—

⬭ tell a story

⬭ explain something

⬭ tell readers to do something

TEKS 2.14A

STOP

41

> ## Read this selection. Then answer the questions that follow it.
> ## Fill in the circle of the correct answer.

The North Wind and the Sun
Adapted by Mary Ann Hoberman

1   I'm the North Wind.
I am cold. I am strong.
No one can beat me
When I come along.

5   I am the Sun.
I am gentle and warm.
That gives me more power
8   Than coldness or storm.

Silly old Sun,
10 You are not very <u>bright</u>!
Let's have a contest
To see who is right.

GO ON

42

Grade 2: Reading Practice

13 Look down below

14 At that <u>bundled-up</u> man.

15 Make him take off his warm coat
   If you can.

Of course I can do that!
I'll raise up a squall
And blow off his coat
20 With no trouble at all.

21 The more that you blow, Wind,
   And show off your might,
   The more the man shivers
24 And pulls his coat tight.

25 Well, you go and try
   Since you think you're so hot!
   But if I can't do it,
   You surely cannot.

   I'll come out right now
30 From behind this big cloud
   And warm the man up.
   Look! He's laughing out loud!

So what if he's laughing
And you're shining bright!
35 He's still got his coat on.
It's still pulled up tight.

Grade 2: Reading Practice

Name _____ Date _____

But look at him now!

Though I don't want to gloat,

I have made him so hot

40   He's unbuttoned his coat!

He has taken it off!

42   You have beaten me, Sun

So I have, silly Wind!

You have lost! I have won!

45   Moral: Blow and bluster do not pay.

46   Gentleness will win the day.

Name _____ Date _____

1 The word <u>bright</u> in line 10 means—

⬭ cheerful

⬭ smart

⬭ shiny

TEKS 2.5B

2 In lines 13 through 15, which words
help the reader know what
<u>bundled-up</u> means?

⬭ *look down*

⬭ *make him*

⬭ *take off*

TEKS 2.5B

3 The Sun's words to the North Wind
in lines 21 through 24 make the
reader feel—

⬭ hungry

⬭ cold

⬭ sad

TEKS 2.7

4 In line 42, the words "You have
beaten me" mean—

⬭ the Sun won the contest

⬭ the Sun kicked the North Wind

⬭ the North Wind is smooth

TEKS 2.11

5 In lines 45 and 46, the moral "Blow
and bluster do not pay" means—

⬭ the North Wind owes money

⬭ being forceful will not help you
get your way

⬭ words are stronger than
actions

TEKS 2.11

6 This selection teaches the reader
that—

⬭ the North Wind causes storms

⬭ people need to wear coats

⬭ you can be gentle and strong

TEKS 2.6A

GO ON ➤

Grade 2: Reading Practice

Name _____ Date _____

7 Read the sentences in the chart.

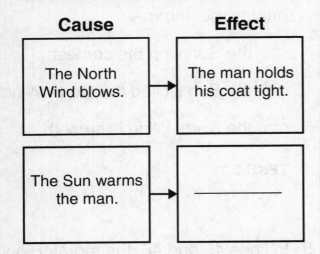

Cause	Effect
The North Wind blows.	The man holds his coat tight.
The Sun warms the man.	_____

Which effect should be added to the chart?

- The North Wind blows the coat away.
- The man shivers.
- The man takes off his coat.

TEKS RC-2(D)

8 The North Wind has a contest with the Sun to—

- win the man's coat
- prove that he is stronger
- raise up a squall

TEKS 2.9B

9 Which line from the poem shows that the Sun has won?

- *I am gentle and warm.*
- *I'll come out right now*
- *He's unbuttoned his coat!*

TEKS RC-2(D)

10 Why does the North Wind want to blow off the man's coat?

- He wants to win the contest.
- He does not like the man.
- He wants the coat for himself.

TEKS 2.9B

11 What is the poem mainly about?

- The North Wind and the Sun have a contest. The Sun wins.
- The Sun and the North Wind do not like each other.
- The man wears his coat because he is very cold.

TEKS RC-2(E)

Grade 2: Reading Practice

Writing a One-Page Composition

Responding to a Prompt

Do you write in a journal? Do you write reports? People use writing every day. It is important to write well, which means:

- Writing about one event or main idea

- Putting your ideas in order

- Building your ideas with details and examples

On a test, you will read a writing prompt. The prompt will ask you to write a personal narrative or a composition. The prompt will include rules to follow when you write. These rules are **READ** or **LOOK, THINK,** and **WRITE.** Make sure you understand the prompt.

Step 1: Plan Your Composition

Put your ideas in order before you write:

- A prompt asks you to write a personal narrative about an important event. Draw a web. Write the event in the center circle. List details about the event in the other circles. Then start your first draft.

- Another prompt asks you to write a composition about how to do something. Use a flowchart. At the top of the flowchart, write your **main idea.** Then list steps in the boxes. Make sure your steps are in order. Do not write more than one page.

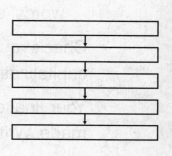

GO ON ➡

47

Name _____ Date _____

Step 2: Draft Your Composition

Use the ideas in your graphic organizer to write a first draft.
You should have a beginning, a middle, and an ending. Use
details to support your main idea.

Step 3: Revise and Edit Your Composition

Reread your draft. Look for ways to improve your writing. For
example:

- Delete sentences that are not about the topic. Add
  sentences that are about the topic.

- Use words that are interesting to the reader.

- End your composition with a strong statement.

- For each type of composition, ask yourself questions:

  - Does every sentence have a purpose? If not, delete
    or rewrite sentences.

  - Is every sentence in the best place? If not, consider
    moving them around.

  - Does my writing seem choppy? If so, change the
    lengths of some sentences.

  - Does my writing flow smoothly? If not, add transition
    words, such as *before, next,* or *then*.

- Check your draft for errors in spelling, grammar,
  capitalization, and punctuation.

- Your final draft should include all of the changes you
  made. Write neatly and no more than one page.

Grade 2: Writing

Name _____ Date _____

Written Composition: Personal Narrative

LOOK

Look at the picture in the box below.

THINK

Surprises are fun! People can surprise us in many ways.

Think of a time when someone surprised you. What did that person do? How did it make you feel?

WRITE

Write a one-page composition about a time when someone surprised you.

As you write your composition, remember to —

❏ write a true story about being surprised.

❏ put ideas in order. Use time-order words.

❏ use words that help show how you feel.

❏ use correct spelling and grammar.

❏ write no more than one page.

Name _____ Date _____

Sample Response: Personal Narrative

Write a one-page composition about a time when someone surprised you.

The writer uses details that support the main idea.

> My dad surprised me when we went to a store. He told me to close my eyes. I didn't know why but I did it. Then I could hear music. My dad said open your eyes. My dad said I could pick out anything I wanted because I had a good report card. That was cool!

The writer uses words that show the feeling of surprise.

> I was so excited! I got to play the keybords and the tamboourine, but I liked the guitars and the drums the most. Dad said You can't have them all! I had to pick just one. But I was still happy. I picked a guitar. It was a great surprise.

Sample Response: Personal Narrative

Write a one-page composition about a time when someone surprised you.

The writer includes an unnecessary detail about a friend.

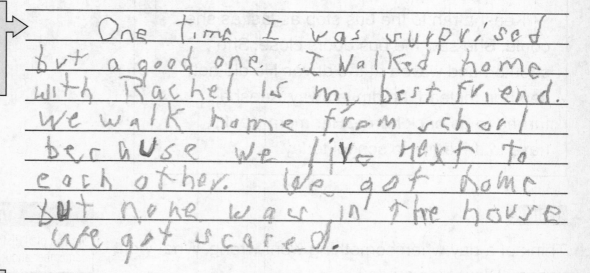

One time I was surprised but a good one. I walked home with Rachel is my best friend. We walk home from school because we live next to each other. We got home but none was in the house we got scared.

The writer confuses the reader by using past and present verbs.

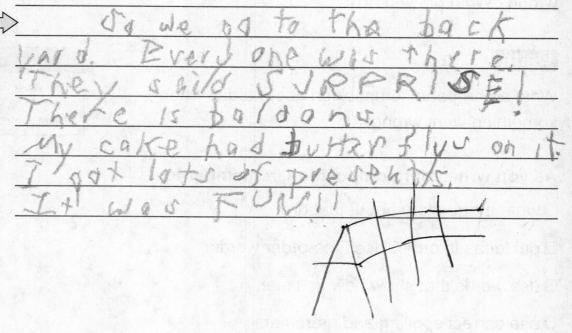

So we go to the back yard. Every one was there. They said SURPRISE! There is boldona. My cake had butterflys on it. I got lots of presents. It was FUN!!

Grade 2: Personal Narrative

Name _____ Date _____

Written Composition: Personal Narrative

TEKS 2.17B, 2.17C, 2.17D, 2.18A

READ

Read the story in the box below.

> Keesha ran to the bus stop as fast as she could. She saw the bus doors close. She shouted and waved at the driver. He did not see her. Instead, he drove away. Keesha turned to go back home. Her mom would have to drive her to school today.

THINK

Think of a day when something went wrong. What went wrong? What did you do?

Tip
As you plan, list what you remember about the day.

WRITE

Write a one-page composition about a day when something went wrong.

Tip
When you revise, make sure all of your sentences tell about what went wrong.

As you write your composition, remember to —

❑ write a true story about that day.

❑ put ideas in order. Use time-order words.

❑ use words that show how you feel.

❑ use correct spelling and grammar.

❑ write no more than one page.

Name _____ Date _____

Sample Response: Personal Narrative

> **Write a one-page composition about a day when something went wrong.**

The writer uses verbs that tell about what happened in the past.

The writer uses words like *first, second*, and *last* to organize ideas.

When I was little I helped my mom make cupcakes BUT something went wrong. It all started when my mom needed some stuff to make them.

First we went to a store to buy ~~them~~ it, I got to hold the monney. Second we got a basket. We got eggs and cupcake mix. My mom let me carry the basket. Last we went to chek out BUT I did not have the money. My mom said I needed to find it so I went back. I looked all OVER. I looked by the milk I looked by the chips. I kept going. THERE IT WAS!! It was on the floor. My mom was very happy. I was too. So we made the cupcakes.

Name _____ Date _____

Sample Response: Personal Narrative

Write a one-page composition about a day when something went wrong.

> The day something went wrong. I lost my tickits for hocky. I looked all over. My mom helped. But no tickits. I had to go back to school to keep looking. ok good. The tickits were at school. Then I all most was late. But we got in the game. My team is the Eagles. The goaly is Greet. The eagles won the game 2-0!

The writer does not tell how she found the tickets.

The writer should capitalize proper nouns like the team name.

Written Composition: Expository

LOOK

Look at the picture in the box below.

THINK

Rainy days may not seem like fun, but they can be.

Think of something fun to do on a rainy day. What is it?
What makes it fun?

WRITE

Write a one-page composition about a rainy day.

As you write your composition, remember to —

❏ write about what to do on a rainy day.

❏ use a topic sentence. Put ideas in order.

❏ build your ideas with facts and details.

❏ use correct spelling and grammar.

❏ write no more than one page.

Grade 2: Expository

Sample Response: Expository

> **Write a one-page composition about something fun to do on a rainy day.**

The writer includes a strong topic sentence.

For something Fun to do on a rainy day try watching the rain. Wait For a storm and ~~su~~ some rain. Watch how hard it comes down. Lots of rain makes puddles. Puddles are Fun to splash in! Wear boots so your Feet don't get wet. But wait till it stops raining.

The writer uses complete sentences to tell about something fun.

Allso you can count the thunder. Watch For ~~th~~ lightening. Lightening is Fast and bright. When you see it then you start counting. Stop when you hear the BOOM! That tells you how Far away the thunder is. It is Fun to count thunder and watch the rain on rainy days.

Grade 2: Expository

Sample Response: Expository

> Write a one-page composition about something fun to do on a rainy day.

The writer does not begin with a capital letter.

if it rains you have to be inside your house. Something fun to do are puppet shows. I have lots of puppets. Sometimes my Gramma comes over and she likes the shows. she all ways claps. Shows are fun if people clap.

I had a puppet show about a fire. the people was scared. But no one got hurt. But the house did get burnt. The fire truck came. A doctor came and a helper. I made a lowd noise for the fire truck. You need to moue when you hear it.

The writer does not include a strong ending.

Name _____ Date _____

Written Composition: Expository

READ

Read the sentences in the box below.

> Many different types of animals live on Earth. Some animals live on land. Some animals live in water. Some animals fly in the air. Every animal is interesting in its own way.

THINK

Think of an animal that is interesting. Why is it interesting?

Tip

As you plan, list ways that your animal is interesting.

WRITE

Write a one-page composition about the animal.

Tip

When you revise, make sure you do not use the same words over and over.

As you write your composition, remember to —

❏ write about the animal.

❏ use a topic sentence. Put ideas in order.

❏ build your ideas with facts and details that explain why the animal is interesting.

❏ use correct spelling and grammar.

❏ write no more than one page.

Name _____ Date _____

Sample Response: Expository

Write a one-page composition about an interesting animal.

The writer explains what makes the animal interesting.

The writer builds ideas with clear details.

Raccoons are interesting animals. They are awake at night. Other animals sleep at night. Raccoons live in cities and in the woods. Some live on my street. Their faces look like they have masks.

Raccoons have sharp teeth. They are wild. Don't pet one!" It could bite you. They have tails with stripes. They can climb lots of things. They can swim. Sometimes they find food in trash cans.

Raccoons are smart too. They know how to get food. Raccoons are interesting because they are different from other animals.

© Houghton Mifflin Harcourt Publishing Company

Grade 2: Expository

Name _____ Date _____

Sample Response: Expository

| Write a one-page composition about an interesting animal. |

The writer misspells the word *giraffe*. This could confuse a reader.

> Animals are very interesting.
> Giraffs are my favorit. They
> have long nehks so they can
> eat tall ~~tall~~ trees. I saw a
> baby giraff at a zoo it was
> so cute!

The writer does not use many details to describe the animal.

> Giraffs are yellow and
> they have brown spots. They kind
> of look like a horse but they
> are so TALL!!!
> I wish I had one.

Written Composition: Personal Narrative

LOOK

Look at the picture in the box below.

THINK

Sometimes we may need help from others.

Think of a time when you needed someone's help. What did you need help with? Who helped you? How?

WRITE

Write a one-page composition about a time you had help.

As you write your composition, remember to —

❏ write a true story about needing help.

❏ put ideas in order. Use time-order words.

❏ use words that show how you feel.

❏ use correct spelling and grammar.

❏ write no more than one page.

Name _____ Date _____

Written Composition: Personal Narrative

READ

Read the story in the box below.

> TJ's teacher passed out the tests. TJ had studied very hard. He hoped he did well. His teacher placed his test in front of him. He got a perfect score! TJ felt very happy. He smiled up at his teacher, and she smiled back.

THINK

Think about something that made you feel very happy. What was it? Why did it make you happy?

WRITE

Write a one-page composition about a time when you felt very happy.

As you write your composition, remember to —

❏ write a true story about feeling happy.

❏ put ideas in order. Use time-order words.

❏ use words that help the reader picture what happens and show how you feel.

❏ use correct spelling and grammar.

❏ write no more than one page.

Name _____ Date _____

Written Composition: Expository

LOOK

Look at the picture in the box below.

THINK

Many adults have important jobs. They might help people
or animals. Their jobs are important for different reasons.

Think of an important job. What is it? Why is it important?

WRITE

Write a one-page composition about an important job.

As you write your composition, remember to —

❏ write about a job that is important.

❏ use a topic sentence. Put ideas in order.

❏ build your ideas with facts and details.

❏ use correct spelling and grammar.

❏ write no more than one page.

Written Composition: Expository

TEKS 2.17B,
2.17C, 2.17D, 2.19A

READ

Read the sentences in the box below.

> Marta was hungry. She went into the kitchen and looked in the refrigerator. She found some apple wedges. Marta opened a jar of peanut butter. She spread the peanut butter on the fruit. She ate her snack. Yum!

THINK

Think of a healthy snack that is easy to make. What is the snack? How do you make it?

WRITE

Write a one-page composition about how to make a healthy snack.

As you write your composition, remember to —

❑ write about making a healthy snack.

❑ use a topic sentence. Put ideas in order.

❑ build your ideas with facts and details.

❑ use correct spelling and grammar.

❑ write no more than one page.

Name _____ Date _____

Revising

After you have finished writing a first draft, your next step is **revising**. Sometimes there are parts of your writing that do not make sense. Sometimes there are ideas that are out of order. Revising means fixing problems like these.

When you revise your writing, you can delete words or sentences that you do not need. You can also add words or sentences to better support the main idea.

Read this chart to learn more about ways to revise your writing.

Check
• Make sure the topic sentence clearly states the main idea.
• Make sure the facts, details, and examples tell about the main idea.
• Make sure you end with a concluding sentence that sums up the ideas.
Add
• Add words, phrases, and sentences that are about the main idea.
Delete
• Delete words, phrases, and sentences that are not about the main idea.
Move
• Move a word or sentence if it would fit better somewhere else.
Sentences
• Use complete sentences that are different lengths.

Name _____ Date _____

Revising

**Read the introduction and the passage below. Then read each
question. Fill in the circle of the correct answer.**

---

*Diego wrote this report about the state flower of
Texas. He needs help revising it. Read his report
and think about the changes he should make.
Then answer the questions that follow.*

Our State Flower

(1) In some parts of Texas, you might see blue
flowers pop up at the beginning of spring. (2) They
grow along roads. (3) They add to fields of grass.
(4) The bluebonnet is the state flower of Texas.

(5) Bluebonnets are named for their shape and
color. (6) Each petal on the flower is like a bonnet,
a kind or type of hat. (7) Bluebonnets can grow.
(8) They bloom from March until May. (9) In May,
the top petals on bluebonnets turn purple or red.
(10) The color change means the flowers will soon
be gone.

(11) The bluebonnet has been a favorite flower
in Texas for a very, very long time. (12) It has been
the state flower since 1901! (13) Every spring,
people look forward to the return of the Texas
bluebonnet. (14) The bluebonnet needs sunshine
to grow.

> **Tip**
>
> Think of details that Diego
> could add to support the
> main idea.

> **Tip**
>
> If a detail does not belong,
> delete it.

Grade 2: Revising

© Houghton Mifflin Harcourt Publishing Company

Name _____ Date _____

1 What change should be made in sentence 3?

  ◯ Add *did* after **They**

  ◯ Add *any* after **to**

  ◯ Add *color* after **add**

TEKS 2.17C

2 Which sentence could **BEST** follow sentence 3?

  ◯ These flowers are mostly blue.

  ◯ These flowers are called bluebonnets.

  ◯ These flowers grow in the spring.

TEKS 2.17C

Tip
Add a sentence when a reader might need more information.

3 What change should be made in sentence 6?

  ◯ Change *Each* to **All**

  ◯ Delete *or type*

  ◯ Delete *hat*

TEKS 2.17C

Tip
If a word or words repeat information, delete them.

4 What phrase could **BEST** be added to the end of sentence 7?

  ◯ next to the house

  ◯ and grow and grow

  ◯ most of the year

TEKS 2.17C

GO ON

Grade 2: Revising

5 Which word could **BEST** be deleted from sentence 11?

⬭ favorite

⬭ very

⬭ long

TEKS 2.17C

6 Which sentence does **NOT** belong in the last paragraph?

⬭ Sentence 12

⬭ Sentence 13

⬭ Sentence 14

TEKS 2.17C

Tip
Look for the sentence that is out of place.

STOP

Name _____ Date _____

Read the introduction and the passage below. Then read each question. Fill in the circle of the correct answer.

Ramona wrote a story about going fishing with her dad. She needs help revising it. Read Ramona's story and look for changes she should make. Then answer the questions that follow.

The One That Got Away

(1) My dad loves fishing. (2) My sister and I enjoy fishing with on the lake. (3) My dad, my sister, and I go almost every week. (4) My sister and I didn't have much luck catching fish the first time we went fishing. (5) Dad helped us bait our hooks. (6) We waited and waited by the side of the lake. (7) We didn't get a single!

(8) Dad said we should find something to do while we waited. (9) He showed us how to skip rocks across the water. (10) The water was cold. (11) We also chased ducks together, too. (12) We had a great time!

(13) When we walked back, one of us had finally gotten a bite. (14) We were too late, though. (15) The fish had pulled Dad's pole and right into the water! (16) Fishing is a fun thing to do, but sometimes the fish win.

1 What change should be made in sentence 2?

⬭ Delete *fishing*

⬭ Add *him* after *with*

⬭ Delete *on the*

TEKS 2.17C

2 Which sentence could **BEST** follow sentence 4?

⬭ Dad said we would get better with practice.

⬭ My sister is pretty good at playing basketball.

⬭ I once found a brand new dollar bill on the ground.

TEKS 2.17C

3 Which word could **BEST** be added to the end of sentence 7?

⬭ wait

⬭ hook

⬭ bite

TEKS 2.17C

4 Which sentence does **NOT** belong in the second paragraph?

⬭ Sentence 8

⬭ Sentence 9

⬭ Sentence 10

TEKS 2.17C

GO ON

Grade 2: Revising Practice

Name _____ Date _____

5 Which change should be made in sentence 11?

⬭ Delete *also*

⬭ Delete *chased*

⬭ Delete *ducks*

TEKS 2.17C

6 Which phrase could **BEST** be added after the words *walked back* in sentence 13?

⬭ walking together

⬭ to our fishing poles

⬭ to chase more ducks

TEKS 2.17C

7 Which change should be made in sentence 15?

⬭ Delete *fish*

⬭ Delete *pole*

⬭ Delete *and*

TEKS 2.17C

8 Which sentence could **BEST** follow sentence 15?

⬭ We hope we will be late getting back again.

⬭ We all learned a lesson from that.

⬭ Fishing is not a fun thing to do.

TEKS 2.17C

Grade 2: Revising Practice

> **Read the introduction and the passage below. Then read each question. Fill in the circle of the correct answer.**

Carlo wrote a story about his family trip to Big Bend National Park. He needs help revising it. Read Carlo's story and look for changes he should make. Then answer the questions that follow.

Junior Ranger

(1) Last summer family visited Big Bend. (2) Big Bend is a national park in West Texas. (3) There was so much to explore! (4) My mom and I once explored the woods behind our neighborhood.

(5) Big Bend is very much beautiful, but it can also be dangerous. (6) I learned how to stay safe in the park. (7) I also learned about the history of Big Bend. (8) I learned about people who once lived in the area. (9) I took photos of birds other animals. (10) I drew pictures of different kinds of plants. (11) I became a Junior Ranger in the park and earned a badge. (12) I felt proud.

(13) I can't wait to visit more and more national parks. (14) I have already told my parents which ones I want to go to. (15) I will become a Junior Ranger at each one I visit. (16) That way, I can teach other people how.

1 Which change should be made in sentence 1?

○ Change *Last* to **Next**

○ Add **my** after *summer*

○ Add **that** after *summer*

TEKS 2.17C

2 Which sentence does **NOT** belong in the first paragraph?

○ Sentence 2

○ Sentence 3

○ Sentence 4

TEKS 2.17C

3 Which word does **NOT** belong in sentence 5?

○ much

○ but

○ also

TEKS 2.17C

4 Which sentence could **BEST** be added after sentence 6?

○ There is a store where you can buy maps of the park and other supplies.

○ A ranger is a person who takes care of the park and enforces its rules.

○ A person should never walk off of the trails or feed the animals.

TEKS 2.17C

Grade 2: Revising Practice

Name _____ Date _____

5 What is the **BEST** way to revise sentence 9?

◯ Add **other** after **of**

◯ Add **and** after **birds**

◯ Add **bears** after **animals**

TEKS 2.17C

6 Which sentence could **BEST** be added after sentence 12?

◯ Becoming a Junior Ranger is not easy.

◯ There are many people who spend the night in the park.

◯ Big Bend is a long way from cities and towns.

TEKS 2.17C

7 Which change should be made in sentence 13?

◯ Add **ever** after **can't**

◯ Delete **and more**

◯ Change **national** to **Big Bend**

TEKS 2.17C

8 Which phrase could **BEST** be added after the word **how** in sentence 16?

◯ to learn about new places

◯ to take photos of animals

◯ to enjoy our national parks

TEKS 2.17C

Grade 2: Revising Practice

Editing

Editing is the next step after revising. When you edit, you look for errors in grammar, punctuation, capitalization, and spelling. The goal of editing is to catch and correct your errors, especially those that may confuse the reader.

Read the chart to learn more about ways to edit your writing.

Grammar

- Make sure you have used all nouns, pronouns, verbs, adjectives, and adverbs correctly.

- Check that prepositions and prepositional phrases are used correctly.

- Check that you have added transition words to put your ideas in order.

- Be sure that sentences have correct subject-verb agreement.

Punctuation and Capitalization

- Make sure apostrophes are added correctly to contractions (*isn't, aren't, can't*) and possessive nouns.

- Check that you have used ending punctuation correctly.

- Be sure to capitalize the names of people and places, the days of the week, and the names of the months.

Spelling

- Use spelling patterns and rules to check your spelling.

Editing

TEKS 2.17D, 2.21A(vi),
2.21B, 2.22B(i), 2.22C(i),
2.22C(ii), 2.23B(iii)

Name _____ Date _____

Editing

Read the introduction and the passage below. Then read each question. Fill in the circle of the correct answer.

Nema wrote directions telling how to make a book of poems. She needs help editing it. Read her directions and think about the changes she should make. Then answer the questions that follow.

How to Make a Book of Poems

(1) This is how you can make a book of poems? (2) First, pik lined paper with holes. (3) This is because you will put yarn through the holes when you are done. (4) Next, write as many poems as you like. (5) You can write about people or animals. (6) You can tell about a place you live or visited. (7) Just writes one poem on each sheet of paper.

(8) Now, put your poems in a piel. (9) Get two pieces of yarn. (10) Put one piece of yarn through the top holes and tie the ends. (11) Put one piece of yarn through the bottom holes. (12) Don't forget to tie the yarn. (13) Your almost finished. (14) Last, show your book to a Friend. (15) You can read the poems together.

Tip
An asking sentence ends with a question mark.

Tip
Some words with a long vowel sound, such as *make* and *line* follow the CVCe pattern.

GO ON

Grade 2: Editing

Name _____   Date _____

TEKS 2.17D, 2.21A(vi),
2.21B, 2.22B(i), 2.22C(i),
2.22C(ii), 2.23B(iii)

1 What change should be made in sentence 1?

⬭ Change *This* to **These**

⬭ Change *make* to **made**

⬭ Change the question mark to a period

TEKS 2.22C(i)

Tip
Use a period at the end of a statement.

2 What change should be made in sentence 2?

⬭ Change *pik* to **pick**

⬭ Change *paper* to **paper's**

⬭ Change *holes* to **wholes**

TEKS 2.17D

3 What change should be made in sentence 7?

⬭ Change *writes* to **write**

⬭ Change *on* to **against**

⬭ Change *sheet* to **shete**

TEKS 2.21B

Tip
Make sure the subject and verb in a sentence agree.

4 What change should be made in sentence 8?

⬭ Change *in* to **in front of**

⬭ Change *piel* to **pile**

⬭ Change the period to an exclamation point

TEKS 2.23B(iii)

Name _____ Date _____

TEKS 2.17D, 2.21A(vi),
2.21B, 2.22B(i), 2.22C(i),
2.22C(ii), 2.23B(iii)

5 What change should be made in sentence 13?

◯ Change *Your* to **You're**

◯ Change *almost* to **all most**

◯ Change *finished* to **final**

TEKS 2.21A(vi), 2.22C(ii)

6 What change should be made in sentence 14?

◯ Change *Last* to **Next**

◯ Change *to* to **too**

◯ Change *Friend* to **friend**

TEKS 2.22B(i)

Tip
Capitalize proper nouns, not common nouns.

Grade 2: Editing

Name _____ Date _____

Editing
PRACTICE

TEKS 2.17D, 2.21A(iii),
2.21A(iv), 2.21C, 2.22C(i),
2.23B(i), 2.23B(iv), 2.23C

> **Read the introduction and the passage below. Then read each question. Fill in the circle of the correct answer.**

Arthur wrote a letter about painting and working in the garden. He needs help editing it. Read Arthur's letter and look for changes he should make. Then answer the questions that follow.

Arthur's Letter

Dear Uncle John,

(1) how is your summer going? (2) I am still using the paint set you gave me. (3) I hope to finish my new painting son. (4) I can't wait to show you the painting the next time you visit. (5) I think you'll really like it?

(6) Do you remember the hedge of flours? (7) We have more flowers this year. (8) An neighbor came by to help with the garden today. (9) We worked quick because it was so hot out. (10) Dad has to keep bringing us cold water to drink.

(11) We have been working really hard to take care of the flowers. (12) There has not been much rain this summer. (13) The flowers need so much water. (14) Everything arond here is so dry. (15) I hope it rains more next year.

Yours truly,

Arthur

Editing
PRACTICE

TEKS 2.17D, 2.21A(iii),
2.21A(iv), 2.21C, 2.22C(i),
2.23B(i), 2.23B(iv), 2.23C

1 What change should be made in sentence 1?

- ⬭ Change *how* to **How**

- ⬭ Change *your* to **our**

- ⬭ Change *going* to **goes**

TEKS 2.17D

2 What change should be made in sentence 3?

- ⬭ Change *hope* to **hop**

- ⬭ Change *my* to **me**

- ⬭ Change *son* to **soon**

TEKS 2.23B(iv)

3 What change should be made in sentence 5?

- ⬭ Change *you'll* to **you**

- ⬭ Change *like* to **likes**

- ⬭ Change the question mark to a period.

TEKS 2.21C, 2.22C(i)

4 What change should be made in sentence 6?

- ⬭ Change *you* to **we**

- ⬭ Change *hedge* to **hedje**

- ⬭ Change *flours* to **flowers**

TEKS 2.23B(i)

GO ON

Grade 2: Editing Practice

Editing
PRACTICE

Name _____ Date _____

TEKS 2.17D, 2.21A(iii),
2.21A(iv), 2.21C, 2.22C(i),
2.23B(i), 2.23B(iv), 2.23C

5 What change should be made in sentence 8?

○ Change *An* to **A**

○ Change *by* to **away**

○ Change *help* to **helped**

TEKS 2.21A(iii)

6 What change should be made in sentence 9?

○ Change *worked* to **work**

○ Change *quick* to **quickly**

○ Change *was* to **were**

TEKS 2.21A(iv)

7 What change should be made in sentence 10?

○ Change *has* to **had**

○ Change *bringing* to **bring**

○ Change *drink* to **drank**

TEKS 2.17D

8 What change should be made in sentence 14?

○ Change *Everything* to **Every thing**

○ Change *arond* to **around**

○ Change *here* to **hear**

TEKS 2.23C

81

Editing
PRACTICE

TEKS 2.21A(ii), 2.21A(v),
2.21A(vii) 2.21B, 2.22C(iii),
2.22B(ii), 2.23C, 2.23E

> **Read the introduction and the passage below. Then read each question. Fill in the circle of the correct answer.**

Maria wrote a story about a trip to the zoo. She needs help editing it. Read Maria's story and look for changes she should make. Then answer the questions that follow.

Going to the Zoo

(1) I realy like going to the zoo. (2) We have a wonderful zoo in our city. (3) It is very large. (4) You cant even see it all in one day.

(5) My class went on a field trip to the zoo monday. (6) We had so much fun on the trip. (7) Last, we went on a long bus ride to get to the zoo. (8) Then, we had to walk with a buddy and be careful to stay with the class. (9) We saw many different animal there. (10) The little spider monkeys was my favorite animals. (11) One monkey was down in a tree. (12) He was hanging from the tree branch by one arm.

(13) The bus was waiting for us when we left the zoo. (14) When we got back to school we all drew pictures of our trip to the zoo. (15) Our teacher put all of the pictures in a class book. (16) Now its there to look at any time we wish.

Editing
PRACTICE

TEKS 2.21A(ii), 2.21A(v),
2.21A(vii) 2.21B, 2.22C(iii),
2.22B(ii), 2.23C, 2.23E

1 What change should be made in sentence 1?

- ⬭ Change **to** to **too**

- ⬭ Change **realy** to **really**

- ⬭ Change the period to a question mark

TEKS 2.23C

2 What change should be made in sentence 4?

- ⬭ Change **cant** to **can't**

- ⬭ Change **in** to **on**

- ⬭ Change **one** to **won**

TEKS 2.23E

3 What change should be made in sentence 5?

- ⬭ Change **My** to **Mine**

- ⬭ Change **on** to **in**

- ⬭ Change **monday** to **Monday**

TEKS 2.22B(ii)

4 What change should be made in sentence 7?

- ⬭ Change **Last** to **First**

- ⬭ Change **we** to **our**

- ⬭ Change **get** to **git**

TEKS 2.21A(vii)

Editing
PRACTICE

TEKS 2.21A(ii), 2.21A(v),
2.21A(vii) 2.21B, 2.22C(iii),
2.22B(ii), 2.23C, 2.23E

Name _____ Date _____

5 What change should be made in sentence 9?

⬭ Change *saw* to **see**

⬭ Change *animal* to **animals**

⬭ Change *there* to **their**

TEKS 2.21A(ii)

6 What change should be made in sentence 10?

⬭ Change *little* to **littel**

⬭ Change *was* to **were**

⬭ Change *my* to **mine**

TEKS 2.21B

7 What change should be made in sentence 11?

⬭ Change *monkey* to **monkeys**

⬭ Change *was* to **is**

⬭ Change *down* to **up**

TEKS 2.21A(v)

8 What change should be made in sentence 16?

⬭ Change *its* to **it's**

⬭ Change *at* to **from**

⬭ Change *wish* to **wishes**

TEKS 2.22C(iii)

Grade 2: Editing Practice

Texas Write Source

Assessments

Name _____ Date _____

Pretest

Part 1: Basic Elements of Writing

Questions 1–10: Read each sentence. Choose the best way to write the underlined part of the sentence. Fill in the circle of the correct answer.

1 Yesterday, we <u>visit</u> the parrots at the zoo.

  ⚬ visiting

  ⚬ visited

  ⚬ Make no change

2 One parrot <u>was</u> bright green and blue.

  ⚬ are

  ⚬ were

  ⚬ Make no change

3 Parrots use <u>its</u> toes to climb trees.

  ⚬ their

  ⚬ they

  ⚬ Make no change

4 Most parrots <u>eats</u> fruit, nuts, and seeds.

  ⚬ eated

  ⚬ eat

  ⚬ Make no change

5 Macaws are <u>large</u> than other kinds of parrots.

  ⚬ larger

  ⚬ largest

  ⚬ Make no change

6 Many parrots make their nest <u>at</u> hollow trees.

  ⚬ for

  ⚬ in

  ⚬ Make no change

7 Parrots are wild animals, <u>or</u> some people keep them as pets.

- ⟶ but
- ⟶ so
- ⟶ Make no change

8 Sally <u>carefully</u> put the food into the parrot's cage.

- ⟶ careful
- ⟶ carefuller
- ⟶ Make no change

9 Sally's <u>Parrot</u> can talk.

- ⟶ parrot
- ⟶ Parrots
- ⟶ Make no change

10 Next week, we <u>makes</u> a book about parrots.

- ⟶ made
- ⟶ will make
- ⟶ Make no change

Questions 11–14: Read each question and fill in the circle of the correct answer.

---

11 Which is a complete sentence written correctly?

- ⟶ My two sisters and me.
- ⟶ Mom and Dad gave us a puppy.
- ⟶ A small, white puppy with floppy ears.

12 Which is the best way to combine these two sentences?

> Our puppy likes to run.
>
> Our puppy runs in the field.

- ⟶ Our puppy runs and likes the field.
- ⟶ Our puppy in the field runs.
- ⟶ Our puppy likes to run in the field.

GO ON ➡

13 Which sentence is a question that should end with a question mark?

- ⬭ We named our puppy Spot
- ⬭ Spot is six months old
- ⬭ How much does Spot weigh

14 Which is a run-on sentence that should be written as two sentences?

- ⬭ Our cat does not like Spot she chases him.
- ⬭ Spot will go to the vet's office next week.
- ⬭ Dad is building a doghouse for Spot.

Questions 15–16: A student wrote this paragraph about a parade on the Fourth of July. It needs some corrections. Read the paragraph. Then read each question. Fill in the circle of the correct answer.

The Fourth of July

(1) On July 4, we celebrated the birthday of our nation. (2) In the morning, we had a parade on our street. (3) This year, I dressed up as Uncle Sam. (4) Sue rode a pony. (5) Juan played the drums. (6) All the really little kids sat in wagons. (7) The wagons were red. (8) We pulled the wagons up the street.

15 What type of paragraph is this?

- ⬭ expository
- ⬭ narrative
- ⬭ persuasive

16 Which sentence is not important and should be removed from the paragraph?

- ⬭ sentence 1
- ⬭ sentence 2
- ⬭ sentence 7

GO ON

Name _____ Date _____

Part 2: Proofreading and Editing

> **Questions 17–24: Read the passages. Choose the best way to write each underlined part. Fill in the circle of the correct answer.**

My <u>famaly</u> took a summer vacation in <u>july</u>. We went to Cape
    17   **18**

Cod. That is part of Massachusetts. At the end of the Cape is

Provincetown. <u>There</u> is a very tall tower in Provincetown. It is
              19

called the Pilgrim Monument. It reminds us of the Mayflower and

the Pilgrims that landed there so many years <u>ago?</u>
                                       20

17 ◯ famly

    ◯ family

    ◯ Make no change

19 ◯ Their

    ◯ They're

    ◯ Make no change

18 ◯ Julie

    ◯ July

    ◯ Make no change

20 ◯ ago.

    ◯ ago,

    ◯ Make no change

GO ON ▶

Name _____ Date _____

July 5, 2011

Dear Kristen,

You are lucky! You are having fun at camp. I'm stuck here at
                                                              21
home. One good thing did happen. My neighbor's cat had kittens.

Mom said that I can have one. We will bring the kitten home soon.

Me and Mom need to go shopping. We will buy a litter box. a food
22   **23**
dish, and some cat toys. I can hardly wait!

Write to me. My sister Sally says, Hi! Come home soon."
                                    24

Your friend,

Amy

21 ⬭ I'am

⬭ Im

⬭ Make no change

22 ⬭ Mom and me

⬭ Mom and I

⬭ Make no change

23 ⬭ a litter box a food dish

⬭ a litter box, a food dish,

⬭ Make no change

24 ⬭ "Hi! Come home soon."

⬭ Hi! Come home soon.

⬭ Make no change

GO ON ➡

Name _____ Date _____

Part 3: Writing   Narrative

READ

You can have fun when you like what you are doing.

THINK

Think of a day when you did something fun. Maybe you went to a special place. Maybe you visited someone you like.

WRITE

Write a narrative composition telling about a day when you did something fun.

As you write your composition, remember to —

❏ focus on one experience—a day that you did something fun

❏ organize your ideas in an order that makes sense, and connect those ideas using transitions

❏ develop your ideas with specific details

❏ make sure your composition is no longer than one page

Name _____ Date _____

Progress Test 1

Part 1: Basic Elements of Writing

Questions 1–10: Read each sentence. Choose the best way to write the underlined part of the sentence. Fill in the circle of the correct answer.

---

1 We read about Christopher Columbus in <u>ours</u> class.

○ our

○ us

○ Make no change

2 In 1451, Columbus was born <u>in</u> Genoa, Italy.

○ to

○ of

○ Make no change

3 Genoa <u>are</u> next to the sea.

○ is

○ were

○ Make no change

4 In Genoa, his parents <u>makes</u> cloth.

○ making

○ made

○ Make no change

5 Many ships brought gold, spices, <u>but</u> silk from Asia.

○ so

○ and

○ Make no change

6 Ships <u>sailed</u> into Genoa every day.

○ sailing

○ sails

○ Make no change

GO ON ➡

Name _____ Date _____

7 For Columbus, the harbor was the <u>goodest</u> place in the world.

- ◯ better
- ◯ best
- ◯ Make no change

8 On a ship, the sailors <u>works</u> hard.

- ◯ work
- ◯ working
- ◯ Make no change

9 The city's <u>street</u> were always crowded with people.

- ◯ streets
- ◯ Street
- ◯ Make no change

10 Carts and wagons moved <u>noisily</u> through the streets.

- ◯ noisy
- ◯ noisier
- ◯ Make no change

Questions 11–14: Read each question and fill in the circle of the correct answer.

---

11 Which is a complete sentence?

- ◯ The large white sails of the ship.
- ◯ Columbus wanted to become a sailor.
- ◯ After he moved to Portugal.

12 Which is the best way to combine these two sentences?

Columbus left Italy.

Columbus moved to Portugal.

- ◯ Columbus left Italy, he moved to Portugal.
- ◯ Columbus left Italy and moved to Portugal.
- ◯ Columbus left and moved to Italy and Portugal.

GO ON

Name _____ Date _____

13 Which is a run-on sentence that should be written as two sentences?

○ Columbus wanted to find a better route to Asia.

○ Columbus sailed across the Atlantic Ocean.

○ He sailed for many days his men searched for land.

14 Which sentence is a question that should end with a question mark?

○ Columbus needed money for his trip

○ The king and queen of Spain gave money to Columbus

○ Did Columbus find Asia or America

Questions 15–16: A student wrote this paragraph about how to dry flowers. It needs some corrections. Read the paragraph. Then read each question. Fill in the circle of the correct answer.

How to Dry Flowers

(1) Flowers are beautiful, but they do not last long. (2) You can save flowers if you dry them. (3) It is easy to do. (4)_____, pick the flower you want to save. (5) Put the flower between two pieces of wax paper. (6) Then put the flower inside a large, heavy book. (7) Close the book and let the flower dry. (8) After a week or two, you will have a pretty, dried flower to keep.

15 What type of paragraph is this?

○ narrative

○ expository

○ persuasive

16 Which is the best word for the blank?

○ Next

○ Last

○ First

GO ON

Name _____ Date _____

Part 2: Proofreading and Editing

> **Questions 17–24: Read the passages. Choose the best way to write each underlined part. Fill in the circle of the correct answer.**

Where is the largest desert in the world? It is in Africa.

The Sahara covers most of North Africa. In fact, it is about the

same <u>sise</u> as the <u>United States!</u> It gets very hot in the desert.
    17   **18**

During the summer in America, we use sunscreen to protect our

skin. People who live in the Sahara cannot <u>by</u> sunscreen at a
                                          19

store. Instead, <u>them</u> cover themselves in long, loose robes.
               20

17 ⬭ size

⬭ cize

⬭ Make no change

19 ⬭ buy

⬭ bye

⬭ Make no change

18 ⬭ United states

⬭ united States

⬭ Make no change

20 ⬭ we

⬭ they

⬭ Make no change

GO ON

<u>Were</u> Having a Party!
21

Come to our <u>party?</u> We'll have <u>games races</u> and food.
22   23

Who: Alex and Joe

When: Saturday, July 9, at 1:00 P.M.

Where: Our backyard

Mom says, <u>"Bring your swimsuit."</u> She is going to turn on
24

the sprinkler!

21 ⭕ We'are
   ⭕ We're
   ⭕ Make no change

22 ⭕ party.
   ⭕ party,
   ⭕ Make no change

23 ⭕ games races,
   ⭕ games, races,
   ⭕ Make no change

24 ⭕ Bring your swimsuit.
   ⭕ "Bring your swimsuit.
   ⭕ Make no change

GO ON ➡

Part 3: Writing   Expository

LOOK

Look at the picture in the box below.

THINK

What can you make to eat? Maybe you can get a bowl of cereal for breakfast. Maybe you can make a sandwich or a salad for lunch.

Think of a meal you can make. Think about what you need to make it.

WRITE

Write an expository composition that explains how to make something to eat.

As you write your composition, remember to —

❑ think about a central idea—how to make something to eat

❑ organize your ideas in an order that makes sense, and connect those ideas using transitions

❑ develop your ideas using facts, details, and experiences

❑ make sure your composition is no longer than one page

Progress Test 2

Part 1: Basic Elements of Writing

> **Questions 1–10:** Read each sentence. Choose the best way to write the underlined part of the sentence. Fill in the circle of the correct answer.

1 Most frogs and toads <u>lays</u> eggs in the water.

    ◯ laying

    ◯ lay

    ◯ Make no change

2 The eggs <u>in</u> the water grow into tadpoles.

    ◯ on

    ◯ at

    ◯ Make no change

3 Is that a toad <u>but</u> a frog?

    ◯ and

    ◯ or

    ◯ Make no change

4 Soon the tadpoles <u>grows</u> into frogs.

    ◯ growing

    ◯ grow

    ◯ Make no change

5 After a few weeks, <u>them</u> can leave the water.

    ◯ they

    ◯ their

    ◯ Make no change

6 A toad's legs are <u>shortest</u> than a frog's legs.

    ◯ shorter

    ◯ short

    ◯ Make no change

GO ON

Name _____ Date _____

7 Last week, Peter and Jane <u>caught</u> frogs in the pond.

- ⬭ catching
- ⬭ catched
- ⬭ Make no change

8 The frogs <u>quick</u> jumped off the rock.

- ⬭ quickly
- ⬭ quicker
- ⬭ Make no change

9 My three <u>sister</u> like to catch tadpoles.

- ⬭ Sisters
- ⬭ sisters
- ⬭ Make no change

10 Tomorrow we <u>swimming</u> in the pond.

- ⬭ will swim
- ⬭ swam
- ⬭ Make no change

Questions 11–14: Read each question and fill in the circle of the correct answer.

---

11 Which is a complete sentence written correctly?

- ⬭ Laying eggs in a pond or brook.
- ⬭ Some frogs and toads jumping.
- ⬭ Tree frogs climb into trees.

12 Which is a telling sentence and should end with a period?

- ⬭ Nearly all frogs and toads eat bugs
- ⬭ Wow, look at that huge frog
- ⬭ Have you ever seen a toad before

13 Which is the best way to combine these two sentences?

> Anna found a frog.
>
> Anna took it to school.

- ○ Anna found and took a frog to school.

- ○ Anna found a frog, she took it to school.

- ○ Anna found a frog and took it to school.

14 Which is a run-on sentence that should be written as two sentences?

- ○ A Darwin's frog looks like a green leaf.

- ○ Some frogs can change color they can hide from their enemies.

- ○ One kind of African toad looks like the bark on a tree.

Questions 15–16: A student wrote this paragraph about how eyes stay clean. It needs some corrections. Read the paragraph. Then read each question. Fill in the circle of the correct answer.

How Eyes Stay Clean

(1) Have you ever wondered how your eyes stay clean?
(2) First, your eyelashes protect your eyes. (3) Eyelashes stop dirt and dust from getting into your eyes. (4) Second, your eyes make tears all the time. (5) They help keep your eyes clean and wet.
(6) When you blink, you spread the tears across your eyes.
(7) Any dust that gets in your eyes is washed away.

15 What type of paragraph is this?

- ○ persuasive

- ○ narrative

- ○ expository

16 Which would be the best closing sentence for this paragraph?

- ○ Eyes are made to take care of themselves!

- ○ Eyes are not the same.

- ○ You should wear sunglasses.

GO ON

Name _____ Date _____

Part 2: Proofreading and Editing

Questions 17–24: Read the passages. Choose the best way to write each underlined part. Fill in the circle of the correct answer.

Every November, we have Thanksgiving dinner with Aunt

Lynette. My mother packs the car on <u>Wednesday</u>. We leave <u>rite</u>
                                          17   **18**

after school. It <u>take</u> about three hours to get to my aunt's house.
              19

When we get there, Aunt Lynette always says the same thing.

She says, <u>"My, how you've grown!</u> The next day, we all sit down
              20

for a great dinner.

17 ○ wednesday

   ○ Wendsday

   ○ Make no change

18 ○ right

   ○ wright

   ○ Make no change

19 ○ taken

   ○ takes

   ○ Make no change

20 ○ "My, how you've grown!"

   ○ My, how you've grown!

   ○ Make no change

Name _____ Date _____

September 24, 2011

Dear Mrs. <u>Smith!</u>
    21

Thank you for visiting our <u>class,</u> We learned a lot about our city.
                            22

We also <u>herd</u> about how we can help others. We did not know that
        23

so many people need food and clothes. Our school has decided

to help. This fall <u>we'll</u> have a Harvest Fair at school. We will give
                    24

the money we make to the Help Our Neighbors Center. Please

come to the Harvest Fair.

       Sincerely,

       Your friends at Wilson School

21 ⬭ Smith.

    ⬭ Smith,

    ⬭ Make no change

23 ⬭ heard

    ⬭ heared

    ⬭ Make no change

22 ⬭ class?

    ⬭ class.

    ⬭ Make no change

24 ⬭ well

    ⬭ we'ill

    ⬭ Make no change

GO ON ➡

Name _____ Date _____

Part 3: Writing   Expository

READ

The playground is a place where you can play with your friends.

THINK

What is your favorite playground game? It might be kickball or four squares. It might be something else.

Think about your favorite playground game. How do you play it?

WRITE

Write an expository composition that explains how to play your favorite playground game.

As you write your composition, remember to —

❏ think about a central idea—how to play your favorite playground game

❏ organize your ideas in an order that makes sense, and connect those ideas using transitions

❏ develop your ideas using facts, details, and experiences

❏ make sure your composition is no longer than one page

Name _____ Date _____

Post-test

Part 1: Basic Elements of Writing

> **Questions 1–10:** Read each sentence. Choose the best way to write the underlined part of the sentence. Fill in the circle of the correct answer.

1 Some birds <u>has</u> wings but cannot fly.

    ◯ have

    ◯ having

    ◯ Make no change

2 They use their wings for balance as they run <u>quick</u> away from prey.

    ◯ quicker

    ◯ quickly

    ◯ Make no change

3 These birds cannot fly, <u>but</u> they are very good runners.

    ◯ or

    ◯ and

    ◯ Make no change

4 The ostrich is the <u>big</u> bird in the world.

    ◯ biggest

    ◯ bigger

    ◯ Make no change

5 Adult ostriches <u>grow</u> to be 8 feet tall!

    ◯ growing

    ◯ grown

    ◯ Make no change

6 A frightened ostrich <u>run</u> away at 45 miles per hour.

    ◯ running

    ◯ will run

    ◯ Make no change

GO ON

7 Most ostriches live <u>in</u> Africa.

○ at

○ for

○ Make no change

8 A penguin's <u>body</u> is made for swimming.

○ bodies

○ Body

○ Make no change

9 Penguins use <u>its</u> wings like flippers in the water.

○ it's

○ their

○ Make no change

10 Penguins <u>slides</u> across the ice on their stomachs.

○ sliding

○ slide

○ Make no change

Questions 11–14: Read each question and fill in the circle of the correct answer.

---

11 Which is a complete sentence?

○ Shawn puts birdseed in the feeder.

○ Large brown bags of birdseed.

○ Watches the birds every day.

12 Which is the best way to combine these two sentences?

Carl makes wooden bird feeders.
Carl makes birdhouses, too.

○ Carl makes wooden bird feeders, he makes birdhouses.

○ Carl makes wooden bird feeders and Carl makes birdhouses.

○ Carl makes wooden bird feeders and birdhouses.

GO ON ➡

13 Which is a run-on sentence that should be written as two sentences?

- ⬭ There are many different kinds of birdseed.

- ⬭ Some birds like thistle seeds other birds like sunflower seeds.

- ⬭ Birds can usually find plenty of food during the summer.

14 Which is a telling sentence that should end with a period?

- ⬭ Don't let the camera fall in the water

- ⬭ Have you seen any seagulls at the shore

- ⬭ My mom likes to watch the birds at the pond

Questions 15–16: A student wrote this paragraph about her cousin's library. It needs some corrections. Read the paragraph. Then read each question. Fill in the circle of the correct answer.

The Family Library

My cousin Sue is lucky. Her parents have a library in their home. The shelves are filled with books. On one wall, there is a huge map of the world. A thick carpet covers the floor. It makes the room very quiet. We can curl up in soft, cozy chairs. _____ we can read all afternoon.

15 What type of paragraph is this?

- ⬭ expository

- ⬭ persuasive

- ⬭ description

16 Which is the best word for the blank?

- ⬭ Third

- ⬭ Then

- ⬭ Before

GO ON ➡

Name _____ Date _____

Part 2: Proofreading and Editing

> **Questions 17–24:** Read the passages. Choose the best way to write each underlined part. Fill in the circle of the correct answer.

People use cloves as a spice. Cloves are used to make baked

ham and ketchup. <u>Theyre</u> also used <u>in</u> many desserts. Cloves
         17   **18**

grow on trees in Africa. But a clove tree does not make flowers

until it is five years old. <u>Befor</u> the flowers open, the farmers pick
                     19

them. The flowers are dried in the <u>son</u> until they turn brown.
                            20

17 ⬭ They're

    ⬭ The're

    ⬭ Make no change

18 ⬭ of

    ⬭ at

    ⬭ Make no change

19 ⬭ Bifore

    ⬭ Before

    ⬭ Make no change

20 ⬭ soon

    ⬭ sun

    ⬭ Make no change

Name _____ Date _____

February 26, 2011

Dear Sue,

I have great news. <u>Mr Peabody,</u> my neighbor, had a yard sale
21

<u>yesterday?</u> He was selling some old children's books. He said,
22

"I have a special deal <u>today!</u> I bought five books for your library.
23

They cost only one dollar. My favorite one is *The Gingerbread*

Man.

I can't wait to see you next week.

Your <u>cousin</u>
24

Amanda

21 ⬭ Mr. Peabody

⬭ mr. Peabody

⬭ Make no change

22 ⬭ yesterday,

⬭ yesterday.

⬭ Make no change

23 ⬭ today!'

⬭ today!"

⬭ Make no change

24 ⬭ cousin,

⬭ cousin.

⬭ Make no change

Name _____ Date _____

Part 3: Writing   Narrative

READ

Learning how to do new things is important.

THINK

Think about a time when you learned to do something new, such as ride a bike or tie your shoes. Who taught you? How old were you?

WRITE

Write a narrative composition telling what happened when you learned to do something new.

As you write your composition, remember to —

❑ focus on one experience—a time when you learned to do something new

❑ organize your ideas in an order that makes sense, and connect those ideas using transitions

❑ develop your ideas with specific details

❑ make sure your composition is no longer than one page